A True Story

Always An Answer

An Inspirational Adoption Story

By Richard Geiger

Table Of Contents

PREFACE

This book is written for two reasons. First, because the story of my adoption helps give encouragement to all people who are adopted wishing to find their natural parents and think it is impossible. Second, to put into words everything I had to go through in order to accomplish my goals. Goals can be obtained. Even goals everyone else tells you are impossible to achieve. Many people over the years asked me to write my story. I have also written this book for all of you. So, sit back and read this unbelievable true story. Please never forget, there is always an answer!

DEDICATION

This book is dedicated to my Mother
Therese Gladieux Geiger, my friend
Renee Monette and to the Blessed
Virgin Mary. Without the help of these
three incredible women this book could
never have been written. Also, to my
Father Tom Geiger for giving me a
family name and the experience of a
father/son relationship. And finally, to
my wonderful son Mikail, who has
taught me joy and the true meaning of
unconditional love. I am so proud of the
man you've become!

DRIVING TO MONTREAL CHAPTER 1

This story started a long time before today, but I have to start it somewhere. This was the day I took action for what I believe was my inalienable right. There were questions that needed answering and I had spent enough time asking the people around me the same questions over and over. What question is that you are probably asking? I wanted to know where did I come from? How did I get here? Why had I been given up for adoption? Most importantly, who were my biological mother and father? I wanted to know whose family's genes flowed through my blood! I telephoned the Canadian Courts in Montreal and asked "What do I need to do in order to find my natural parents?" The woman answering the telephone told me it would be best to come up there in person. Filing a court request regarding my adoption was the only way to make this happen. In November 1976, I just voted for the very first time in the United States.

I was 20 years old and driving in my Dodge van from La Salle, Michigan to Montreal, Canada. I had my Ohio driver's license on me and an U.S. NATURALIZATION certificate with the name of Richard Joseph Geiger. I also, had a Canadian passport issued January 1957, which included a baby picture of myself at five months of age under another name. As I was driving over the Ambassador bridge in Detroit, I recalled my Mother telling me the story of how she and my Dad brought me into the U.S.A. through the Windsor Tunnel late at night. An elderly U.S. Immigration Officer stamped my passport. My parents told me they took the tunnel late at night, because my Canadian Health papers stated I was exposed to the chicken pox. My parents were afraid I might be quarantined but I wasn't. My passport was stamped January 1957. I was going back to Montreal where I was born, determined to find those answers. It's always interesting to hear how a person found out that they were adopted.

Some people find out early on. Others when they become adults. Some people are never told that they were adopted. I found out early on, when one day my childhood friends Steve Madras, Tracy Myers and I was playing like all kids do. We were arguing over which game we wanted to play. Steve was outvoted and he got mad and said to me, "I am going home!" I remember Tracy and I teasing him a bit more, then he yelled at me "Yeah Ricky, well you're adopted, so there!" I knew he meant something bad by the way he said it. I thought I had heard that word before, but I didn't know what it meant. Since he had used this word in a negative context, I was very curious as to what this word meant? I remember asking Tracy and she just looked at me as puzzled as I was. Tracy was four years old. I was five. Steve was seven months older than me, so perhaps a little ahead of the game. I went into my house and asked my mother, "What is adopted?" I knew I had said something I shouldn't have, because the surprised look on her face said it all.

She asked me right away, "Where did you hear that?"

I told her what Steve had said. She right away spoke,

"Well, there are lots of people that are adopted" and

named several friends of the family. Then I asked,

"Is Steve adopted?" She said, "No!"

I asked, "Is Tracy adopted?" She said "No!"

It's at this point I felt different from my two closest

friends. Later that night my Mother and Father sat

both my brother Tom and I down and talked about us

being adopted. I went to bed thinking about how

I came from another woman's "tummy" and that she

couldn't keep me. We were fortunate because some

parents have children and don't get a choice what

baby they get. They got to choose and they had

chosen Tommy, my baby sister Gigi and myself.

We were special. For the next five years, I wondered

about who my "real mother" was and felt a real

sadness around my birthday. It's almost as if l could

pick up on her pain of missing me. Wanting to know

where I was, if I was okay? I wanted to know if she

was okay and why had she given me away.

I would ask my Mom from time to time if she knew anything about my "real mother." I could tell that it upset her, because she would always say to me, "but I am your Mother." Looking back on it now, it was probably very hard for her to deal with my questions. I never meant to hurt her by asking. I only wanted to find out what happened to my "real parents." As I continued driving towards Montreal, I was recalling how my parents took our family to Montreal to see "EXPO 67" World Fair.

It's July 1967 and I remember it well. The U.S. pavilion all made up in this beautiful plastic round glass dome. It was spectacular! At the U.S.S.R. pavilion, I can still remember smelling these canisters to guessing what was inside of them. I was very excited to be in the city where I was born. While we were there, I kept asking my parents if we could see where Tommy and I came from. My sister was adopted from Ohio, but my brother and I both came from the same place, St. Jacques Creche De Misericorde.

Tom and Terrie Geiger received my brother Tom in late August of 1954. My brother was never really interested to go and see or to know where he came from. Nevertheless, my parents kept their bargain with me and we went to the place I was born.

I remember seeing the large dorm style rooms with hundreds of babies crying and waiting to be fed. My Mother started to cry. We all said let's take one home. I remember my Father saying that we only came to see where you boys came from and that we are the family that we are and that was it! It sounded very logical to all of us and soon after that, my Mom stopped crying. It was sad to see all those babies in those rooms without parents. I felt very lucky leaving there that I was "chosen" by the Geiger's. Just before we left, I asked one of the catholic nuns if I could know where my real mother was. She laughed saying, "you can never know!".

I asked, "Why?" Again, the nun answered in the same manner. I can remember thinking how can she say that I can never know?

I knew that I would find out someday, somehow.

I knew this nun was wrong, I just knew it! While we were in Montreal my Mom took us to a huge church called St. Joseph's Cathedral. It was breathtaking overlooking all of Montreal and beyond. We were allowed to pick any alter to light a candle at to make a wish/prayer. I chose the Blessed Virgin Mary's statue right away. I figured if anyone could help me, she would. As I lit the candle I remember praying to Mary if she could just let me find my mother while I was in Montreal, because I didn't think that I would ever be back there again. For the next few days I kept looking at women around the age of thirty thinking she could be my mother. I left Montreal a little sad that I didn't get to meet my real mother and a little upset with Mary too. At least, I had seen where I came from. That brought me great comfort, but I will never forget seeing all those babies lying there, waiting to be chosen. It seemed a few more years went by, but always around my birthday I could feel my real mother's sadness, wanting to know where l was.

Starting High school at fourteen, one of my first

assignments was to learn how to use their library.

While I was there, I looked up information on my

Grandfather Gladieux my Mom's dad. He lived near

us in Toledo and was sort of famous in the town.

I read tons of information about him, which was

fascinating I could write a whole book about this

man. Virgil Gladieux was a great person. I am

honored to have had him as one of my male role

models and as my loving Grandfather. All of my

Grandparents Virgil and Beatrice Gladieux, Ben and

Dorothy Geiger, were kind and loving people.

As I was going through this information about Virgil,

I saw an article about him from 1959. Next to his

article was another stating that the United States

Government was no longer requiring Canadians to

show their passports to enter the United States.

A Canadian driver's license would be enough at the

end of 1959. I went home that day and stormed into

the house to ask my Mom where my Canadian

passport was. She seemed stunned and acted as if she

did not know what I was talking about.

My Mom had always been bad at lying, because she hardly ever did it! I could always tell when she wasn't forthcoming and this was one of those rare times.

Then I thought about where she would keep it. I knew she had a key in her office desk for a safety deposit box at the bank. That is where it had to be.

I went into her office and took the key from the drawer. I showed her that I had the key and that if she did not take me to the bank, right then and there that I would go without her and cause a scene.

I told her she could open it up to prove to me my Canadian passport was not in there. I think my Mother knew at that point the time had come for her to tell the truth. While she drove us to the bank, we didn't talk the entire time. We went in together.

She opened the box threw the passport at me and said, "I hope you're happy!" You know what?

I was more than happy. I was ecstatic! Inside was a picture of me as a baby. I had never seen a picture of me that young before. I had these huge eyes, but they were mine. I saw my real name was Gerald Joseph La Fortune.

I was silent for a while and my Mom said, "Let's go home." I kept looking at the picture going home. My Mom said she wanted to wait until we were adults to give us those passports. There was no stopping me, so what could she do? She could tell how happy I was. I thanked her for taking me to the bank. I was really lucky to have the Mom that God had chosen for me. My Mom was kind, fun to be with and her laughter truly contagious. She explained that they changed my name from Gerald to Richard. My brother's name was Thomas Jr. and my Mom's nickname for Therese was Terrie. So, if they had kept my original name it would have been Tom and Terrie, with their sons Tommy and Jerry. With the cartoon characters Tom and Jerry being so popular at that time, there was just no way they were going to call me that. I thanked her and agreed that Richard was a better choice. We both laughed at that moment. She said she kept Joseph because that was the name the orphanage gave to all of the boys. I went to bed that night on cloud nine, where I remained for weeks! After all, I had my original birth name.

As I continued driving towards Montreal, I passed

Toronto and realized that I was getting far away from

home. I was starting to get nervous thinking should

I turn back? Suddenly, I remembered this song that

I knew and had heard several times over the past few

years. I started to sing it and it kept me going.

When I was 19 my Dad took me to Europe for one

week. We went to Rome and Paris. Europe was so

exciting to see! It was truly an unforgettable father

and son trip. On our flight back home, we flew over

Montreal. The pilot announced that you could see

Montreal very clearly from the left side of the

aircraft. The side where I was seated. My Dad looked

at me and said "See Ricky, that's where you came

from, remember?" I put my headphones back on and

what song came on at that exact moment? 'Rikki,

don't lose that number' by Steely Dan. I remember

looking down and thinking you must go there and

find her. This song is proof I am supposed to go and

find my biological mother. I didn't feel any sadness

coming from her on that day in October 1975. I knew

we had to find one another again.

I was the only one who could do it!

I would like to say at this point, that I know how lucky I was to have been adopted by the Geiger's. They were a young couple, who wanted to give some unfortunate children a better chance in life. My search for my biological parents was something burning inside of me. I never meant it to be taken as an insult by the Geiger's. After all, they had given all three of their children every opportunity to grow up in a wonderful learning environment. My parents were good people, but I still had to do what my heart was yearning for. That was to find out the truth about my heritage.

MEETING RENEE MONETTE CHAPTER 2

Finally, I arrived in Montreal. I decided to stay
somewhere downtown and ended up at the Holiday
Inn. It was close to the area where I would be able to
find my birth information. Waiting for the morning
to come, seemed like forever. I called the orphanage
first thing and asked if l could set up an appointment
to speak to someone regarding my adoption.

The person at the other end asked me what I wanted
to know and that they could not tell me my mother's
name. I would have to file a petition with the courts
to get my records opened. I was told that I could find
out information on my family history if my birth
mother had left any. Some do and others don't,
I was told firmly. I made an appointment with the
adoption agency to meet with them in two days.
I then called downstairs to the front desk and asked,
"Where is the Provincial Court House?" The Palais
de Justice was very easy to find.

An hour later I spoke to a woman in charge of
directing people to where they needed to go at the
Government Information Desk. It was right in the
middle of this huge room. At least it seemed huge to
me, since I was totally lost as to where to go.
The woman's name was Renee Monette; an attractive
middle-aged lady with beautiful, white-gold-blond
hair. It turned out she was the same woman who
answered the phone, when I had called from the
States. She remembered my phone call. Had it not
been for Renee, I am sure I would not have found my
biological mother to this day. Mrs. Monette could
not have been more helpful. She explained how
everything worked in regards to petitioning the courts
to hear my case. With everything written mostly in
French it was difficult. Renee helped me get all the
necessary forms filled out to the best of my abilities.
If l came back in the morning, she would help me
with the rest. I didn't know what to say except to
thank her for all of her help. She asked me where
I was staying and I told her.

She told me to check out in the morning and stay
with her family, because the Holiday Inn would be
expensive. She said she had a son around my age and
that his name was Rick too! I wanted to object, but
she explained I would have to be in Montreal for at
least three or four more days to get everything
processed. The Holiday Inn would eat up all the
money, that I had brought with me. She made clear
I would need my money for other costs I hadn't
thought of. I agreed to come back the next day.
I headed for the birth records division next. There
was a long line of people wanting copies of their
birth records. There was this huge election going on
in the Province of Quebec and it seemed everyone
wanted to vote. Hence, the need for copies of birth
certificates. I watched the people in front of me and
as I was waiting in line. I wondered if l could I pass
myself off as a normal everyday citizen? Could I just
show her my Canadian passport like everyone else?
Why not? When it was my turn, I walked to the
counter said 'bonjour' as best as I could and handed
her the request form and my Canadian passport.

The lady took them, looked and gave the passport back to me. She kept my request form. I watched her walk over to these huge drawers along the wall and pull my birth records. She came towards me sort of tired from the day. Right when she went to hand me the information, she saw something written on my file. She looked at it again. Then, within inches of my hand she clasped it in her arms and said something to me in French. I immediately said in English that those we're my birth records. I had the right to have them. She looked shocked that I spoke English. I yelled at her to give them to me! Another woman came over and they spoke for a few seconds. The second woman apologized and explained they were unable to give me this information. My birth records were private. There was nothing they could do. I said, "Come on, you have them in your hand, I just want to see them." I was told to leave their office immediately or they would call the police. It wasn't worth getting arrested over but I yelled at both of them, "YOU HAVE NO RIGHT TO KEEP THIS FROM ME!"

Everyone in line stared at me. They waited for me to

leave, so I did. The next morning, I checked out of

the Holiday Inn. I went to meet the only person

I knew and had come to trust so quickly, Renee

Monette. She was working the information desk. Just

like the day before, helping hundreds of people each

day. I wondered why she was helping me so much on

this? I gave her all the paperwork I had filled out.

I made copies of everything exactly like she had told

me. I could tell she was happy to see me. Also, she

was delighted, that I had done what she asked.

I said, "Why are you helping me so much and letting

me stay at your house? What if l am a murderer or

something?" She laughed very hard and said "Son,

with those kind eyes and your good manners, I don't

think you are going to murder my family. Besides,

my son is a lot bigger than you are, so I am not

worried." I felt stupid for saying such a thing to her

but it reassured me that she was okay too! Over the

next few days we finished all the paperwork and she

made sure it was filed correctly for me.

While filing my petition, Renee discovered that my

passport had been stamped January 1957. In Canada

babies were not supposed to be given up for adoption

until they were six months and one day old.

My birthday being August 15th it made me only five

months old. I requested the courts to explain why this

had happened and that if there was a chance that my

mother had come back for me. If this was the case,

they would have to give us each other's names and

addresses. This was all in my petition to the courts.

It was exhausting to go through the paperwork

process. I was so relieved when the work was

completed. I could never have done this without

Renee's help. They told me the court would have to

review my case within seven years. Renee Monette

lived in Laval in a modest, clean twin-home.

She shared it with her husband Guy and her son

Rick. Her two older daughters Johanne and Susie,

lived next door in the other half. Renee's family was

fantastic, full of life, laughter and love! I really liked

her son Rick.

I knew we would be friends for the rest of our lives,

no matter what happened with my search.

Rick Monette was two years younger than I was and

really into hockey. Over the next few days, I hung

out with him and his friends. I got a real flavor of the

life of a Canadian teenager living in Laval.

Renee's entire family was so kind and genuine,

I felt very lucky to have met such a kind, loving lady.

C.S.S.M.M.   CHAPTER 3

CENTRE DE SERVICES SOCIAUX DU MONTREAL METROPOLITAIN

I woke up in the morning and prepared to go see

the orphanage people. Renee already notified me

what information they would probably give me.

My mother's age, if she had siblings and what

hobbies she had. She said, "Don't expect more than

that out of them, especially if it's true your mother

came back for you before the six months were up.

I asked her if she thought she had come back. Renee

said, "If she did and you were let go early, that

you're back asking questions will make them very

nervous." Walking up to the place that had given me

away, gave me a very strange feeling.

I thought about what they really knew and what they

were really hiding from me. They had all the

answers to my questions in this building.

I met with a woman by the name of Yolanda
Dunberry. She was very professional and seemed to
know what she was saying. She escorted me into a
little room and asked if l would like something to
drink. I said, "No thanks. What I would like is
information regarding my family history. She
explained that she wanted me to sign a form stating
I would not find the Agency liable for giving me this
information. I asked her why that was necessary?
She replied, "It's just a formality required to release
the additional information." I thought at this point
she was hiding something. I signed the paper
anyway, even though I didn't know what I was really
signing. Mrs. Dunberry left for a moment, then came
back with a file on which some words were
blackened out with a marker. Although I was unable
to read them, I did see the name Octavie printed on
it. I asked Yolanda who Octavie was. She seemed
surprised and looked at the folder. She stated that
was my mother's name and that I should not have
seen that.

In the folder were two pictures one of my Dad
Thomas Geiger and one of my Mom Therese Geiger.
They looked so young; they were around 22 when the
pictures were taken. Also included was a copy of
payment to the Catholic Church as a donation for
their children. I asked Mrs. Dunberry about the
money and she said that back then $10,000.00 was
donated to the Church. There were two plans offered
by the Catholic Church at that time.

The first, three children over a five-year timespan,
including two girls and one boy. The second plan
was two boys within a three-year-period. My parents
applied for two boys. She said there was a bigger
demand for boys than girls back then. I kept thinking
that the Catholic Church had sold me. It was at this
point I brought to Mrs. Dunberry's attention the fact
I was released before six months. I could see in her
eyes, that I had hit a nerve. She was too prepared for
her answer. She right away said, "Lots of babies
went out earlier because of chicken pox outbreaks."

I said, "But what if my biological mother came back for me before the deadline of six months was up?" Her voice quivered and she said,

"Usually if the mother changes her mind it's right after she had her baby. Not after five months of no contact.". I asked her, "So, then you've had no contact with her in those five months?"

She looked right at me and said, "No we haven't." I then asked her quickly, "After I was gone have you had any contact with her before the six-month period was up?" Again, her voiced quivered as she said, "Of course not." but she made a big mistake this time when she said this to me. She did not look into my eyes. She looked down, sort of away from me.

I knew right then and there she was hiding something. Again, I felt it throughout my entire body. I knew she was feeding me misinformation.

I asked her, "Then why was my mother 19 years old when I was born as stated on this birth certificate. Yet on this adoption release form it shows my mother as 20 when she signed me over to your agency?"

She answered that question very fast and said some girls took a few days to think it over.

My mother's birthday was August 20th since I was born on the 15th she turned twenty on the 20th she signed the papers ten days after my birth.

I asked her if the mothers spent time with their babies to breastfeed them. She said, "Oh no, the mothers do not have any contact with their own babies." I said, "Well, then what did my mother do here for ten days?" Her reply was the young girls would help with the cooking, cleaning and attending to each other while staying there. She said this to me in a really sweet voice. Don't get me wrong this lady was really nice and I liked her. I could tell that she liked me too, but for whatever reason, I sensed that her hands were tied. Yolanda promised me she would look to see if there was any other information on my family history. She said she would send me a letter by the beginning of the New Year (1977). That was only six weeks away and it was very nice of her to offer this to me.

I thanked her for her time and left feeling they were definitely hiding something. You cannot imagine all the things I thought they could they be hiding! Perhaps they were hiding that I was stolen, or maybe that I was born from a nun. They would never want anyone to know that the nuns where making and selling some babies themselves. It was torturous, until I cleared my mind and it came to me my mother had come back for me. I thought that the Catholic Church hadn't called the Geiger's to tell them that the Agency had made a mistake and the Geiger's would have to bring me back. It would be easier for the Church to tell a 20-year-old girl you waited too long. Now, your baby is gone. I returned to the Monette's that evening. We spoke about what had happened at the Agency. Now it was just a matter of waiting. I asked Renee again if she thought it would really take seven years to hear my case? She replied, "You can count on it!" Later that night, I went out with Rick and his friends. I watched him play hockey. These guys played tough. Hanging around with Rick the next few days was fun.

Had I grown up Canadian, this was the kind of life I would have had. One night we went to an auto show. While we were inside the arena, my van was robbed. All that was in my van, was a leather jacket that my Dad had bought for me in Rome and my camera case. Unfortunately, my Canadian passport, my U.S. Naturalization papers and the rest of my traveler checks were in it. Half of my checks were from American Express. The other half from a bank in Ohio, that could not reimburse me until I returned to the United States. American Express replaced my money the very next morning.

The saying, 'don't leave home without it!' truly brought its meaning home. The other checks were worthless to me at that time, because I almost didn't have enough money left to get back home. I am sure that the Monette's would have helped me with this problem too, but I was glad that I didn't have to ask them for money. To this day I only buy American Express traveler's checks.

It was sad to lose my original passport, with the only baby picture I had. I had put in all the necessary paperwork and didn't really need the information anymore. I could get another U.S. Naturalization Certificate after returning back home. The morning I was getting ready to leave Montreal, I drove up to St. Joseph's Cathedral with Rick. I told him I wanted to light a candle for good luck, so we both lit candles by the Virgin Mary statue. This time I was more realistic. I just asked Mary to help me win my case and let me find my mother. I left Montreal content and happy with the information I had uncovered. My biological mother's name was Octavie. I was told she was a nurse and 19 years old when I was born which was not true I found out years later she worked in the Kitchen. Her birthday was five days after mine, which made us both Leos. My father was 21, a taxi driver who enjoyed sports and music. Both were French Canadian, in good health and had come from large families. I had filed the necessary paperwork to get my case heard and possibly had to wait seven years for a response. I was looking forward to a letter from Yolanda Dunberry in the coming year. I felt very satisfied having accomplished my goals. It was sad to say good-bye to the Monette's. I knew I would see them again, but I didn't know when. We hugged and kissed each other good-bye. I couldn't have thanked them enough. Words will never be able to express my gratitude and love towards all of them. What a fantastic family Renee Monette had! When I arrived back in Michigan, my roommates Carolyn and Doug informed me they had told my Mom where I went, because she had called all that week for me.

In one way this was good, because I didn't have to break the news to her myself. I did go and see my parents to tell them what I had been doing.

They were a little surprised, but not shocked at all. My Father said if I ever left the Country again, he would appreciate a call first to know where he could find me in case of an emergency. They were both pretty cool about what I had done. They must have thought, "Okay, he has the information and now his search is over."

In January 1977, I received a letter from Mrs.
Dunberry as promised. In it was the following
information dated January 4, 1977.

"Dear Joseph,

*I have finally received from our medical
department the few missing details about your
natural parents and your birth. Please find
enclosed the copy of your file to which I have
added those. I hope everything will be to your
satisfaction and I wish you a happy New Year.
Yolande Dunberry, t.s.p. "*

When I moved to California on my 21st birthday
with Tracy Myers later in the same year, I took the
letter with me and I still have it today. There
wasn't any more information in the letter she sent
me, than what I had already seen when I was in
Montreal. I really felt the letter was sent just to
pacify me. I thought, " I must wait for the Judge's
decision."

MOVING TO CALIFORNIA   CHAPTER 4

Moving to California was one of the best decisions
I had ever made in my life. Living in a city on the
Pacific Ocean was a dream come true for me.
I was finally around people who were progressive in
their thinking. You see, since I was a small child,
I have had psychic premonitions, but I didn't know
what to make of them. I knew these experiences were
unusual for someone to have and if I brought the
subject up to my family, they would just laugh about
it. My Mom would say, "Don't tell people this kind of
stuff. They'll think you're crazy!"
Living in San Diego however, I was able to meet
many other psychics. I even took classes on the
subject after finishing my undergraduate studies.
One of the most exceptional teachers I had, was a
woman by the name of Dr. Betty Jane Poage.
In her classes, I was able to learn how to help others
by using my psychic gift. I learned from her classes
that I was indeed a psychic.

From that day I knew my strength in searching for

my biological parents, came from my psychic

connection with my birth mother. This kept me

going. I realized when I would feel her pain around

my birthday every year, I was really picking up on

her. I knew she was out there sending me these

emotions. She needed to know that I was alive and

well. I wasn't imagining her pain and concern every

year it was real! This connection gave me the

energy to not give up hope of finding her. I can't

fully explain what psychics do, or how they do it.

The best way to describe it is that I am like an

antenna and the energy comes from an invisible

space. Somewhat in the same manner as radio and

television waves. I clear my mind of all thoughts.

Then the information regarding the person

I am channeling for comes to me. Sometimes it

comes in words, sometimes in symbols or pictures to

clarify the message to that particular person.

Over the years I have become fairly good at

channeling and have been able to help many people

along the way.

One of the greatest joys I've experienced through channeling, is being able to assist couples having trouble conceiving children. I give them the necessary information through channeling that enables them to finally get pregnant even in a few cases, to adopt children. I've never charged anyone for my help. I feel that psychic abilities are a gift from God. Since it comes free from God to me, I pass it on to those that need it. Although many psychics do charge for their services, I don't pass judgement on them for doing so. I have chosen not to charge anyone for my assistance. Through word of mouth, I have been able to help dozens of couples all over the world over the years. It has brought me great joy, a couple calling to say following the instructions of the channeled message worked. A few times I have been asked to be the Godfather. One couple let me assist in the actual birthing process. It was really something to see a baby being born right before my eyes, it is truly a miracle!

A couple from Germany even named one of their

sons after me. I have only offered my services when

asked for assistance. I have always kept rather quiet

about my psychic abilities. The world is filled with

people who want to use it for personal gain.

There are also many non-believers regarding psychic

phenomena. I decided to include this in my story, because

it's important to me to let my readers know where I got my

strength. Being a believer in the power of the mind and

soul and knowing that we are all connected somehow,

kept me going! While we're on the subject of psychics,

I want to share with you two experiences that I've had.

One day at work I received a phone call from a friend.

She asked if I would come to a special party in Del Mar.

It would be hosted by a well-known psychiatrist who

worked in La Jolla. I asked her what kind of party it would

be? She replied, "A spoon-bending-party!"

She had been asked to invite any psychics that she knew

in the area. I told her that I would definitely be there!

Upon attending this party, I was given a spoon.

I was informed that this was an experiment in

telekinesis.

We formed a circle and held our spoons or forks. We were supposed to send energy through our minds to the object in our hands and tell it to bend. At first many of us laughed about it, as standing there telling a spoon to bend, did seem a bit strange. However, I suddenly felt energy coming down my right arm. My spoon started to get warm in my band, so I took my left hand and wrapped the spoon up in a spiral. I was amazed and so were the others in my circle. Not long after that their spoons and forks began to bend too. We started laughing with excitement. After all, I had never seen anything like this before.

As I had been the first person to make it work, a very sweet, elderly man walked up to me and asked me if I could do it again for him. So, I did it and gave him one of the wrapped spoons. He told me that he had come there that night, because he felt there is a connection between telekinesis and healing energy. He thanked me and I asked for his name. He said, "I'm Jonas Salk.".

I just about fell over, showing something like this to a brilliant man, who had saved millions of lives with his polio vaccine.

I was a little nervous at that point and apologized for not knowing more on the subject of telekinesis.

Dr. Salk was extremely kind to me. He coaxed me to continue using my psychic abilities, saying, "It is clearly a powerful tool." Then I was given a big steel bar. It took a few minutes, but I was able to bend it a little in a boomerang shape. The man in charge of the experiment wrote down my name and took my picture for his photo album. Then he gave me a button that said, 'certified warm former' on it. I enjoyed the experience of that evening but getting the encouragement from Jonas Salk was the true gift I received that day. That a man as respected as Dr. Salk believed in me, had given me the assurance that being a psychic was a good thing and that I should do more with the abilities God gave to me. The second experience happened a few years later. It was April 10, 1992. I was visiting my relatives in Michigan and Toledo, Ohio for the baptism of my cousin Virgil Gladieux II. I was asked to be his Godfather and I was thrilled.

The baptism was set for April 12th • I flew to Detroit on

the 10th to have dinner with my friend Chris Wenzler

and two of his friends Paul and Joyce, at a restaurant

located on the campus of Wayne State University.

A piece of bread that I had bitten into, suddenly began to

expand in my throat. I took a sip of my beer. Then the

bread blocked my throat completely and I choked.

Chris said, "Are you okay? You're turning blue?"

I couldn't talk and passed out into my soup bowl.

I remembered everybody rushed out of their booths.

One of them tried to shake me, but nothing

happened. Suddenly, I saw a black woman run over,

look at her watch and check me for a pulse.

I didn't have a pulse, nor was I breathing.

I thought, "Why is everyone hovered over my

body?" I saw myself lying on the floor. I looked

totally grey and lifeless. All of a sudden, I realized

I was dead and I started to yell, "Oh my God,

I am dead!" No one could hear me or see that

I was hovering above them in the room.

I said, "Hey, I'm up here!" but everyone kept

looking at my body, lying on the floor.

I got panicky and repeated, "Oh my God,

I am dead!" Then this voice came from out of

nowhere. I turned around and realized that

I was completely out of my body.

I was just a little being of light. I could turn 360°

instantly without a problem. The voice told me to

relax. I wasn't scared, just unsure to where I was.

This voice continued to communicate with me.

It said, "Congratulations you have learned love!"

At that moment I felt a wave of love and warmth

surrounding me. I had never felt as happy and

content as I did at that moment. I asked where I was.

Was I dead? The voice continued to communicate

with me very fast. As soon as I thought of a

question, the answer was given to me. I was told

I had a choice and that not everyone got one. I could

choose to come home or go back to the earth school.

The choice was mine but I had to do it then, as

I could not be out of my body much longer. It would

be too late.

I saw myself swimming in the ocean, bodysurfing and playing the piano and immediately said, "Okay, I want to go back to earth." I asked if I would be loved on earth if I went back? The voice responded by saying, "It's important that you show and teach love while you're on earth and to worry about being loved is not what is important."

I told the voice I understood. Then it was like a vacuum cleaner sucking me back down into my body. I then puked all over myself and the floor, everyone standing over me stated, "He's back."

I then asked about the black woman who was trying to help me. My friends wondered how I knew about the black woman, as I had been unconscious while she was there. I said I had seen all of them working on me. She had been looking at her watch. It turned out she had been eating near our table. She was a nurse and had been timing how long I went without heartbeat or respiration. According to my friends, I was dead for one minute and thirty-four seconds. I had no recollection of the time frame.

I clearly remembered the incident and being in

another dimension, unlike anything I had known

before. I was shaken up for the next few minutes

and I asked Joyce what was going on. She said they

were waiting for E.M.S. to arrive.

I said to her, "But Joyce, I don't have P.M.S.".

Everybody laughed and said, "Ric not P.M.S.

E.M.S.!" I said, "I don't have E.M.S. either".

Joyce informed me that in Michigan the ambulance

service is called Emergency Medical Services.

I was clearly disoriented, but I stood up and felt very

wobbly. I went back to my friend Chris's home and

rested the entire next day. On April 12th

I showed up at the church in Toledo. I was early and

the only one in the church. As I sat there looking up

at the main altar, this feeling came over me about

what had happened to me two days before.

I kept looking up knowing there is life after death!

I made a list of things, I still wanted to do while

I was on earth, after this happened to me.

It included going to Europe to visit Assisi and Rome

again.

I also decided the next time I was in Montreal,

I would look up my natural father. I felt very

fortunate to have been given a second chance to

live. I have kept my promise to teach and show

love. This is why I am sharing this story with you.

It is important that all of us teach and show love.

Remember that everyone is here for a purpose.

I conclude by saying I am not afraid to die.

It's easy, living and loving is the hard part! Moving

to California and learning to deal with my psychic

abilities have proved very helpful over the years.

I knew in 1983 my case would finally be heard after

seven years. I was going to find my natural mother.

The Canadian Courts would not let me down.

I truly felt that justice would be served!

THE COURT'S DECISION CHAPTER 5

1983

I had lived in San Diego for almost six years and had graduated from the University of California San Diego. I was employed by a non-profit agency, that helped ex-offenders find employment. With the unemployment rate at more than 15% in San Diego, my job was both challenging and rewarding to me.

I had not forgotten however, it was the year the Canadian Government would have to review my case. I could hardly wait. Since I had left Montreal in November 1976, I had spoken to the agency three times. Once in 1977 thanking Yolanda for sending me the letter as promised. The second time in 1978 after moving to California telling them to continue using my Mother's address in Toledo, which they already had. Lastly, in 1981 to giving them my permanent address. A P.O. BOX of all things! Now it was the beginning of 1983 and I knew my case would have to be heard within the next twelve months.

I called the Agency and asked for Yolanda Dunberry.

She still worked there, which I could hardly believe.

She thought it was funny I called her at that time. She

was just going over the list of up-coming cases. My

case would be coming up within the next six to eight

weeks. "Perfect timing!" I thought. I gave her both my

home and work telephone numbers and asked her to

call me. She agreed that she would, as soon as she had

received more information. I received a call from her

several weeks later, that my petition had been granted.

The Agency had been given a year to locate my

biological mother, to see if she would want to meet

me. I was so thrilled, I could not believe my ears,

I had actually won! I let out a scream so loud, you

could hear me throughout the entire building.

Everyone ran into my office, because they thought I

was being mugged by one of my clients. Just for the

record, I have never been hurt by any of my ex-

offender-clients.

To this day, I still believe that everyone is entitled to a
second chance. I wished I could have kissed and
hugged the Judge for having done the right thing!
"There was fairness in the Canadian Courts."
I thought to myself.

1984

Almost a year had passed and I received a call from
the adoption agency.

They stated the Agency had been granted an
additional year, because of backlogged searches for
mothers. It seemed that the Agency had been
swamped with court cases and lawsuits.

I was extremely upset but thought "What is one more
year?" Besides, I was probably not the only person
who had won his case and had a mother out there,
somewhere. So, I did nothing about it until the
following year.

1985

In 1985, I called the adoption agency a few weeks
before their deadline. I told them if they asked for
another extension, I would file a lawsuit against
them for purposefully slowing down my case. Five
days later, I received a phone call from a Louise
Bertbrand. She told me she had located my
biological mother. She most definitely
wanted to meet me. I started to cry with tears of joy!
Whenever, I think of this moment in my life, it
makes me cry. My mother actually wanted to meet
me. She had not rejected the opportunity. I knew
how lucky I was. Many people do reject the
opportunity. Almost nine years had passed since I
filed my petition. It seemed like a life time ago.

THE AGENCY'S STORY CHAPTER 6

Louise said she remembered my mother from
1956. Louise had just started out in social
service work and one of her first cases was
my mother's. She continued that she could not
tell me any of this due to privacy regulations
before having spoken to my mother. After all,
my mother had given birth to a child out of
wedlock. Louise told me that the name
Octavie had been made up, while she was in
the orphanage. Most girls used fake names,
she said. My mother's real name was Diana
Chiasson, but now she was married, went by
the name of Diane instead of Diana.
Her last name was now Rochon. I was twenty-
eight years old and I finally knew my mother's
complete name, Diane Chiasson Rochon.
I asked her how I got the name La Fortune.
Louise said the birth mothers picked their
child's name, as long as it wasn't their real
family name.

48

Sometimes it was a message.

I guess mine meant good fortune or good luck. Then I remembered that on his passport my brother Tom's name was La Chance.

Louise said we should write each other a letter and include a recent photo. Louise was very polite about what she was about to say "Richard your mother was in my office and her lifestyle and yours is very different".

I asked her what she meant. Diane apparently came from a pretty tough side of East Montreal. One of her sons had been with her and he had tattoos and long hair. Her son had even brought her on his motorcycle.

"I mean don't get me wrong", she continued "they were very nice. It is just that your world and hers are worlds apart."

I said, "Well, I like long hair on guys." and even though I didn't have any tattoos myself I didn't see the problem. She then said, "Well, I'm afraid they could be members of some gang.

Even your mother has a tattoo on her

shoulder." she went on to say.

I laughed, I knew what she meant. I was well

aware however, that long hair and

motorcycles doesn't equate to bad people. It

may add up to trouble in some people's eyes,

but not in mine. I told her how I felt about

what she had said. We spoke about it quite in

depth. She only looked out for the welfare of

ALL parties involved, including me.

I respected her concern and honesty from her

perspective. I agreed I would write a letter and

include a picture. Louise continued to say my

mother had come back to get me after five

months and 28 days. I had already gone.

Apparently, my mother had wanted her baby.

The Agency had told her that it was too late.

They had not heard from her once, since she

left in August of 1956.

Diane had said that she had six months.

What happened? The nuns told her, there had been

this chicken pox outbreak. Some babies had been sent

out of the country, some to France, others to the

United States of America. There was nothing they

could have done; her baby had been one of those that

went to another country. Diane punched the nun right

in the face, resulting in a black eye and a broken nose.

She had left that day weeping in the arms of her

brother Gerald and his wife. So, I had been right.

She did come back for me. I was speechless! What

this poor, young girl must have gone through, she had

come back for me and I wasn't there. I knew my

search all these years had not been just for my peace

of mind, but even more so for Diane's. Louise told me

Diane had five children, four boys and one girl. Wow!

I had five new siblings. All I thought at that point

was, "Wow!" Louise told me my mother had left the

father's name blank. Louise explained that

I came from another man, other than her husband.

The Agency had no name to give me. I told Louise,

I would come to Montreal in August to meet my

mother. I would call her when I was there, to tell her

how everything was going. She wanted us all to meet

at the Agency first, but I told her it depended on how

my phone calls went with Diane prior to me flying up

there to meet her in person. I had really heard about

enough from this Agency. After all, to me St. Jacques

Creche De Misericorde should have called the

Geiger's in February 1957 to tell them they must

return the baby. The biological mother had come back

for me, before her deadline was up! The Geiger's

should have been given another baby. This is where

fate came in. It was obviously fate to be raised a

Geiger because that was how it turned out to be.

Right or wrong, it really did not matter anymore

because I was all grown up. The Geiger's were the

only family I had ever known.

I am a Geiger what can I say!

FIRST CONTACT BY MAIL CHAPTER 7

I waited for my mother's letter to come to my

P.O.Box. it arrived June 14, 1985. For the very first

time, I was going to see a picture of what my mother

looked like. I was with my boyfriend David Moldt.

We decided to go to the ocean three blocks away, to

open it there. I sat down on a huge rock overlooking

La Jolla Cove and my heart was pounding with

excitement. I could hardly wait the walk. David asked,

what she looked like. I gave him her pictures to look at

first. I wanted to read her letter before looking at them.

Diane basically explained to me in her letter, what the

Agency had told me. David said to me, "Wow, you

really look like her!" I said, "Okay, give me the

pictures, I'm ready." There was this beautiful-looking

woman and we did look alike. She seemed as if she

could be my older sister more than my mother, she

looked so young.

I let David read her letter.

We both got teary-eyed while we watched the sunset over the Pacific Ocean. I looked up into the sky and thanked God for my good fortune.

It was a moment, I will never forget!

June 7, 1985

"Dear Ric, this morning Louise Bertbrand called me at 11 o'clock and said Mrs. Rochon I've just received Richard's letter for you and I said at last my God was I happy. Thanks, Ric, for your letter and for your picture you are a good-looking boy. You look like my family I mean the (Chiasson's) because you know my name before my marriage was Diana Chiasson. Me too I send you a few pictures of my children my husband and I. So, Louise Bertbrand told me this morning that you will be able to come to Montreal around the 20th of August. Yes, Ric it's my birthday and you my dear it's the 15th. I hope to see you this summer. Louise told me too you are looking for me for 8 years. Poor Richard since nearly 29 years me I've been praying the good Lord to see you even just one time before I die.

So, this year is my lucky year. The last time I been kissing you was 10 days after your birth they gave me the permission only one time before I left you there for always. But my heart was crying that day. I asked the good Lord to forgive me with hope to see you one more time before I die and this morning when I see your picture, I give you a big kiss on your picture. Everybody been saying he's nice mama your son. You know Richard my family name is Rochon my husband 's name is Harvey and the names of my kids are Ronald 22, Alain 20, Richard 19, Colette 18, Andre 13. but there's only Andre who lives with my husband and I. Now my dear Richard after the 25th of June my new address will be, we are moving June the 24th so any time my dear Ric you want to come to Montreal at my home you're welcome and don't worry everyone here is anxious to know you. Please Ric excuse my English, please answer me again and try to speak to me about your family. Don't you speak French a bit? So, you will be able to learn here. Bye, bye my dear with all my love, Your Mother Diane XXX,".

I received two more letters from Diane before I flew to
Montreal.

July 2, 1985

"My dear Son, how are you? I hope you feel fine, for me
and my family everybody is okay. I am a little tired
cause you know we are in our new apartment now but I
am glad I love it here. It's made a big change because
we use to be 7 in the house and now, we are only 3.
Dear Ric, in about 48 days you and I will be together
for the second time of our life imagine. I am so happy
when I think about that beautiful day. Last Sunday I
went to my brother Gerald who lives in Laval and he
ask me if l had some more news of you? I said no and he
said I hope that he won't change his mind to come to
Montreal in August. I said I hope because there's too
many peoples here who wait for him. Well Richard
your room is already fix for you. It's not a Holiday Inn
but you will be comfortable here. Ric, I been missing
you so long and now I am so happy you'll never know.
Please Ric, send me just a few words if you don't like to
write often, just to tell me the real date you will be here.

I like to be this time the first one to meet you and bring you at my home. My husband is so happy that I am and all my sons and daughter. I'm telling you the truth everyone told me they are happy to have a brother like you. Now I close my letter and don't forget you have to write me before you come in Montreal okay dear. Your mom who love you Richard, I give you a big kiss XXX."

Then a third letter came in the mail for me.

July 3, 1985

"My dear Son, I sent you a letter yesterday and I received one of you today and I answer immediately, because I don't want you to believe that your letter has been lost. So, now I am sure that you come to Montreal at my birthday. Thank you Richard I never had a more beautiful gift for my birthday in my life. Listen Richard, you told me that "perhaps that we could have lunch together" I will love too, but I want you to be like the other of my children. You come to Montreal to see me, my husband and all of your brothers and your sister. Remember my son, you are my son as well as Ronald,

Alain, Richard and Andre. You all got my blood, you understand? Even if l never take care of you when you were small, you always be in my mind and always will be too. I love you as much as my other kids, okay darling? You know what I mean.

My husband said to me, he thinks that you are just like his own sons for him, because you belong to me and I belong to him. So, there's no jealousy here we are all close to one another. Before you had one family, now you are a lucky man you got two family. Since I found you Ric, I also found a real paradise on earth. I'm so happy you couldn't know. I know you love your parents, your brother and your sister and I'm happy for you and I love them too, because they been good for you. Even if I don't know them, but the blood that flows in you is mine. Now you don't have to feel guilty about all that. I'm the one who's guilty but that is the circumstances of life. Well now I finish my speech, let's talk about California. No, my dear I never went to California it's very far from here, very expensive too. Maybe, I'll go before I die. It must be wonderful, because sometimes I look at the T.V. and look at the baseball games who come from

California and I like to see the San Diego

Padres when they play with Montreal Expos.

Please Ric don't feel sorry about all I have told

you in this letter okay? Because, I want you to

know how much we love you and hope to see

you as soon as possible. Take good care of you

dear and write or call before you take the

airplane okay?

Love and kiss your mother Diane XXXXXXX"

As soon as she had received her new phone number

after moving in July of that year, I called her. It was

July 14th that we finally spoke to each other on the

phone. Mostly, we talked about our need to find one

another. She thanked me for having tried so hard all

those years, instead of giving up on finding her.

I knew she was a good person from the first time

I spoke to her. I had to wait only one more month,

until my vacation time became available. It didn't

seem like much to wait another month. I had worked

on this for years. Diane's letter had some

grammatical errors as you can see but I thought not

bad for someone whose native language was French.

OUR FIRST MEETING-DIANE'S 49th BIRTHDAY
CHAPTER 8

August 20, 1985

Our first meeting was like a dream. Apparently, the original building where I had been born, was torn down. On the location where it used to be, was now a hotel. She wanted us to meet, exactly where she had left me 29 years before. I walked into the lobby. There she was, my mother, she was beautiful! She was nervously standing there in a dark blue sleeveless dress. I saw from a distance she had a tattoo on her shoulder. After that I only saw tears. It seemed time stood still for so long. She told me she had prayed that we would see each other again. She gave birth to me around 4:40 a.m. She was supposed to push a button so the nuns knew she was in labor. She had heard from the other girls the nuns put a sheet up, so the girls were unable to see their baby when it was born. She wanted to see me, so she went through the entire process without calling for help. She said my shoulders were really big and I got stuck.

She pushed the button for help and the nuns came

in. They yelled at her for not telling them sooner.

A radio was playing down the hall, when she was in

labor, Diane told me the song that was playing at

the time I was born, was Elvis's 'Love Me Tender'.

Of all of Elvis's songs it had always been my

favorite. It's the only Elvis's song I learned to play

on the piano. I asked her who my father was and she

said that it didn't matter. But, it did to me.

I told her for the day to continue, she'd have to tell

me. She said she could not bear to say his name.

I told her to write it down on a piece of paper.

I went to get her a piece of paper and a pen.

She wrote down the name Julian La Plante.

We left the hotel lobby. Her husband Harvey was

waiting outside, in their rather vintage styled

station-wagon. I thought, "I do not even know these

people." I had no idea where I was going, except to

their apartment for dinner to meet my four brothers

and one sister. On the way there, Diane and Harvey

spoke French. It sounded so beautiful to me, even

though I only picked up two or three words.

I tried to remember the names of my siblings,

Ronald, Alain, Richard, Colette and Andre. At least

remembering that one of their names was Richard,

was easy. We arrived at an older neighborhood

located on the east side of Montreal. I saw

apartments buildings like this before but had never

gone into one. Growing up in the suburbs really hit

me at that moment. All I wanted was to run away,

because my emotions over-whelmed me to say the

least. Being in a foreign country to meet my birth

mother and her family, everyone speaking French

and this small but very clean apartment was too

much to take in at one time. I thought I was going

to faint several times throughout the evening,

because my head was spinning. We sat down for

dinner. I was starving from flying all day. I ate some

delicious split pea soup with French bread.

As time passed, Diane kept asking if l wanted some

more soup. I said, "Okay, a little more"

I did not want to make a pig of myself before the main course was served. After a little while trying to communicate with my new found family,

I wondered why dinner was taking so long.

My sister Colette brought out a birthday cake with Diane's and my name on it. I realized that the soup had been dinner and this was dessert. The delay between the soup and the cake was the break after the meal. I ate three pieces of cake thinking

I had a lot to learn about how other people lived in the world. The lady at the Agency had been right, their world was very different from mine.

Diane insisted that I stayed with them and not a hotel. We only had six days to spend together so I agreed with her. It really was great to fall asleep each night knowing that I had finally found my birth mother and was a guest in her home. Everyone treated me wonderfully! It was like being in the twilight-zone even though it was reality. It felt as if this wasn't really happening. The next day I would meet my Uncle Gerald (Diane's older brother) who I was named after.

Gerald was Diane's older brother.

I fell asleep thinking the Rochon's were like the
Monette's, a family filled with love and laughter.
I liked all of them! August 21, 1985, I went with
Diane and Harvey to meet Gerald, my namesake
and my Uncle. Gerald and Genie had been married
for 29 years and they were still in love. They had
four beautiful daughters. One of them was named
Gigi, just like my sister in Toledo. They were really
nice people. All of them welcomed me with open
arms and hearts. The first thing Gerald said, was,
"You almost were my son." I was puzzled and
looked at Diane. It seemed that when she was
pregnant, she confided in her brother.

Genie had been his girlfriend at the time, but a few
months after I was born, they got married. They
agreed with Diane they would raise me as their own,
provided Diane was willing to become my Aunt.
She agreed, because she didn't want her baby to be
raised outside of her family. At least this way she
would be able to see me grow up and know what
was happening to me.

In February 1957 before Diane's six months were
up, they had gone that day to bring me home as their
son, but I was no longer there. Not only was Diane
suffering that day, so were they. Gerald said to me,
"Because I had four girls you always were the son
that got away." He asked me if I knew about my
father yet. I said Diane had given me his name,
Julian La Plante. He replied, "Yes, I spoke with him
after you were born, but he denied the whole thing."
Gerald told me he punched Julian for what he had
done to his sister. I said, "Well, he was probably
really scared about what had happened."

We didn't talk about Julian again. I didn't feel the
need to deal with my father at that time. It was hard
enough to cope with meeting my mother and her
family on this trip. I already was so overwhelmed
with meeting so many people. Diane had a really
big family. A few days later, my nephew Steve
Rochon was born. I was very happy for my brother
Ronald, it was his first child. The whole week was a
celebration.

One good event after the other. The night before

I left for California, I took Diane and Harvey out to

dinner with the Monette's, so they could meet.

I wanted my mother to meet the lady, who was

responsible for helping me find her.

This dinner was like a dream. I only remember we

ate Chinese food. The rest of that night was a blur.

Had I bitten off more than I could chew? It didn't

matter, I knew I had done the right thing.

This wonderful lady deserved to find me again

regardless the effect it had on me. Then came my

last day. It was a sad morning, because I could tell

Diane didn't want me to fly back home.

She knew I had a life somewhere else, so she tried

not to show her sadness too much. Before I would

leave, Diane wanted to take me somewhere.

I said sure, where? She said it was a church she had

gone to on my birthday every year to light a candle

for me. My birthday, August 15th is a catholic

holyday, The Assumption of the Blessed Virgin

Mary.

Diane told me she lit a candle there each year,

hoping I was okay and that God would bring me to

her again. I hardly believed she took me to the alter

of the Blessed Virgin Mary at St. Joseph's

Cathedral. I had gone there before in 1967 with my

Mom and again in 1976 with Rick Monette. St.

Mary looked down on me with all these candles

burning below her feet. My mother and I stood there

together. I started to cry, because I knew that all of

this would not have been possible without Mary's

intervention. I held my mother's hand and we lit a

candle together. We had both gone to the same St.

Mary statue over the years and made the same

requests to this holy woman. Our prayers had clearly

been answered. Had it been Divine Intervention or

just good luck? I had no doubts! I thanked Mary and

my mother and I dried the tears from our eyes.

Most of my relatives took me to the airport. We

hugged and kissed good-bye. I told Diane she would

have to come to California someday to see where

I lived. Later that evening, I flew from Montreal to

Detroit, Michigan.

I had to tell my family what had happened, before they heard it from someone else. I didn't even tell my family I had won my court case back in 1983. I wanted to wait until I had actually met Diane before telling them. In a few short hours I went from east Montreal to the comfort zone of my own family. I had pictures of my biological family ready to show them. My parents were a little surprised at first, because I hadn't mentioned about my search again during the past nine years. I reminded them of the time, I had to wait for the courts to hear my case. I could tell they were not that happy about the entire situation. They let me show them the pictures however, and tell them what I had found out.

My Father asked me if I had contacted my biological father as well? I said I hadn't felt the need to do that yet. I had only wanted to find Diane. Two days later I flew back to California. My best friend Dr. Lenny Okun had planned a surprise party for me, welcoming me back home. It was quite the celebration all of my friends were there to greet me.

Everyone wanted to look at my photos from

Montreal. It was great receiving that much support

from my friends! I called Diane about four or five

times a year. We also wrote each other on holidays

and exchanged birthday greetings. I didn't want to

intrude on Diane's life to much, as of all of her

children were still rather young. In 1989 Diane and

my Aunt Genie were finally able to fly to California

to visit me. They both came to see where I lived.

A friend of mine owned a Limo service in La Costa.

I picked them up from LAX in one of his Limos, to

make their trip unforgettable. All three of us had a

fantastic time seeing the sights of San Diego.

I wanted Diane to see I had a perfect life, so she

would never worry about me. I wanted her to see

I was happy. All of my friends came from all over

California just to meet her. Diane had never asked

me who I was dating. I figured if she really loved

me, she would accept whomever I chose to date.

I had discovered I am bisexual, to love a woman or

a man came very easily to me. The subject had

never come up with Diane.

I thought she would find out I have a boyfriend, coming to California. The first night Diane and Genie were there, I had called my roommate, "Honey!" Both Diane and Genie had looked at each other. I simply stated I loved and dated whomever I wanted. I hoped she was okay with this. I explained that my parents in Toledo never really liked that I was gay. They were more "the- don't-ask-don't-tell"-type of people. I told Diane I hoped her love for me would be greater than her concern about my sexuality. Diane immediately said she accepted me for who I was. Even if l had been a cripple in a wheelchair, she would have wanted me as her son! She asked if l had ever had girlfriends. I said "Yes, plenty of them. It is just that I know I am attracted to men more." I could tell both Diane and Genie were surprised to find out David and I were lovers and not just roommates. From that day on, it was never an issue with her or any members of her family. They truly loved me unconditionally! What more could a person ask for from their family.

The fact that I am bisexual didn't change a thing.

We had a fantastic time together, we went everywhere. One day Diane picked a beautiful pine cone off one of my trees. She painted parts of it with pink nail polish and gave it to me as a present. I still have it on my dresser. Genie had brought me some handmade, green ceramic pieces for my green glass collection. She had made them herself; I see them every day in my menagerie case. When the day came for them to fly home, there was a big hole inside of me. I didn't know when I would see Diane again. Once again, I had to put my trust in God to watch out over her. I parked my car near the end of the LAX runway. David and I watched their jet take off. It flew out over the Pacific Ocean and turned back heading east, until they disappeared into the clouds.

JULIAN LA PLANTE   CHAPTER 9

In 1992 I went to Germany to visit a friend who
lived there. I fell in love with the countryside and
decided to visit again in 1993. I ended up moving to
Germany in 1994. I gave Diane my new numbers
and address. I told her that I would keep my post
office box in California, because I would still live
there some of the time. She would not lose track of
me. Diane moved about once every year for one
reason or another. We always kept each other
informed of our whereabouts, though it was great
that we could call each other whenever we wanted
to. One day in June of 1998 I received a wedding
invitation from my brother Andre in the mail.
He already had four children with his girlfriend but
decided to get married. He wanted ALL of his
brothers at his wedding. I checked and it was
possible for me to go. I thought, "Well, if I am going
to Montreal, I should probably look up Julian La
Plante while I am there".

It had been thirteen years since I met my mother.

I was ready to meet the other side of my family too.

I spoke to my friend Rick Monette and told him of

my plans. He gave me the name of a reliable private

investigating company located in Montreal called

Chartrand La Fraboise. The private investigator was

extremely professional. He made sure I wasn't some

crazy guy out to hurt some man who fathered me.

The investigator spoke many times on the phone to

me. We e-mailed on several occasions.

Before giving me any information, he wanted to

contact the Monette's for a reference.

I was quite impressed by his integrity, checking on

my character. Rick Monette spoke to him several

times. I had received Julian La Plante's address and

phone number, before I left Europe for Montreal.

Julian was married and lived out by Parrot Island.

He had owned a taxi company, which he recently

sold to the largest driving school in the area.

Rick picked me up at the airport. I was really lucky

to have such a great friend.

He always took the time to help me out. We called Julian first, instead of just showing up at his front door. When I started looking for my biological parents, I decided not to get in the way of their existing lives. I thought his wife wouldn't know about me. I wasn't out to ruin someone's marriage. We drove out to Parrott Island. As we approached Parrot Island, we realized there was a festival in town. I attempted to call Julian, but there was no answer. We decided to have a beer at the festival. The people of Parrot Island were extremely friendly we had a great time. We decided to come back the next day to find Julian's house. I would attempt to call him again in the morning, before my brother's wedding. I wanted to see Julian's house before I made the call. We found his house without a problem. A very lovely home nestled on a little hill surrounded by a lot of land. It looked like a one-story home from the front, but two stories from the back. I was very nervous to make this call. My heart was pounding just like when I made the first call to Diane.

Even worse, because I didn't know if Julian even

knew I existed. Rick dialed Julian's phone number

for me and handed me his cell phone.

A woman answered. I asked if Julian La Plante was

there. She asked who was calling

I said, "Richard Geiger, an American!" There was a

pause and I could hear her speaking French with

someone Julian came to the phone.

I said, "Mr. La Plante, my name is Richard Geiger.

Does the name Diana Chiasson mean anything to

you?" "Whom?" he asked. I said, "Diana Chiasson,

she was a girl who worked at St. Anne Bellevue

Hospital in 1955. Mr. La Plante, I hope that you are

sitting down, but I have every reason to believe that

you are my biological father." In a very Loud and

clear voice he said, "WHAT?" I quickly said that

I didn't want anything from him. My search for my

natural parents had led me to his door.

I mentioned my Uncle Gerald accusing him of

getting Diana pregnant and hitting him back in

August of 1956. "Do you remember that, I asked?"

He said right away, "OH YES, but I assure you that
I am not your father. If l were your father, then
I would have taken responsibility for it!
There is a big mistake here. You must go to your
mother and tell her she must know that I am not
your father. Does she know that you called me?"
I replied, "No!". He said, "Well, please ask her again
and tell her you spoke to me directly and I am sure
that she will have to tell you the truth."
I didn't know what to say. I asked him if he had
known Diane back in the 50's?
He said, "Yes, but we were only friends. I gave her a
ride to and from work. I assure you when the truth
comes out you will find I am not your father!"
I thanked him for his time and said I would let him
know what I found out. I hung up the phone.
Rick and I just looked at each other in disbelief.
Either Diane is a liar, or this man was truly in denial.
On my way to the wedding I kept thinking,
"Who is telling me the truth?" Diane didn't have any
reason to lie about my father. Julian had many
reasons to deny it!

Yet I felt that Julian was telling me the truth, because

he had said "If I was your father then I would have

taken responsibility for it!" I realized I was more

inclined to believe Julian's story. He didn't deny my

Uncle Gerald punching him, nor knowing Diane.

"What was going on here?" I asked Rick. He said

"Well, one thing's for sure, someone is being

dishonest to you about this. We just have to find out

who it is." Family weddings were always fun for me

to go to. In Toledo, my parents had lots of friends

and relatives, so I had lots of practice at weddings.

I actually met relatives on my mother's side who

came as far away as New Brunswick.

I was not going to bring up Julian La Plante that day.

I had never been to a French wedding before.

It was very provincial, but very relaxed.

There were two couples getting married at the same

time. It was different to see people get married this

way. Listening to two lovers saying their wedding

vows in French, sounded so much more romantic

than in English.

The next day, we were all going to meet at my
brother Richard's home out in the country for a
family barbecue. My sister Colette, her husband
Alain and their two children Marie Eve and Francis,
picked me up from my hotel. I didn't mention Julian
on my way to the family get together. However, that
day was the perfect time to ask Diane the truth!

I had a great day with my relatives. We played
horseshoes and told jokes. It was really a beautiful
day. I didn't know when to bring up the subject
exactly, so I went for a motorcycle ride with
Richard. When we came back Diane was standing
outside by the front door. We had a moment alone,
so I said to her, "Guess who I talked to yesterday?"
She said, "Who?" I said, "Julian La Plante!"
Her eyes opened so wide; I could hardly believe it.
She asked, "What did you talk to him for?"
I told Diane; I had wanted to pay him a visit while
I was there. He told me, he was not my father and
that she wasn't telling the truth. I asked Diane
if she'd been lying to me all these years.

She didn't know what to say to me, there was just

silence. I said, "Why would you tell me Julian is my

father, if he isn't?" She said she didn't want to talk

about it. I said, "Okay, but until you do, you won't

hear from me or see me ever again!"

I left Richard's house really upset, to say the least.

I told her if she changed her mind to call me at the

Sheraton hotel in Laval. I spoke to my sister Colette

about what had happened and why I was upset with

our mother. Colette said, "She will tell you the truth.

Just give her a little time." "A little time"

I said. "For thirteen years I thought Julian was my

father and now I want to know the truth!"

The next morning, I received a call from Diane.

She said "I have written you a letter. You can come

to my apartment and get it if you want. After you

read it, if you still want to talk to me, I will be here."

I called Rick and he took me over to Diane's.

Taped to the door, was a letter that read, Richard

Geiger, Confidential. I took the letter and went back

to Rick's car to open it.

The letter was dated for that day August 3, 1998.

"A letter for you my son. First of all, for the first time since November 4, 1955 I will say you all the truth and I swear on my mother's head this is all the real truth, nothing but the truth.

All started by a letter that I received from my dad on November 4, 1955 he told me that the boyfriend I had at that time want to get married with me. In spring 56 and he want to give me an engagement ring for Christmas 55 and my father told him to stay out of my life he doesn't like him and he would not give him my address in Montreal and he wouldn't give me his address too. He told Diana you better not see him in Montreal because I will go fast to get you and you will have to move back to New Brunswick. So, I was so desperate and confused that in my room in Perrot Island I call a taxi of course it was La Plante. He went and I told him to bring me to Canada Hotel in Ste. Anne of Bellevue he said what are you going to do there?

I said I want to meet two of my girlfriends who

work with me. But it wasn't true. I only wanted to

go there to drink and drink and try to forget the

letter of my dad. So, when I been in the hotel La

Plante was not with me I was alone and at a table

I saw a man who's also alone with his glass.

I knew him because he worked with me in the same

ward in the same hospital than me.

He said hello Diana you're alone I said yes, he

said you want a drink I said I will drink all night.

Then he said why do you have troubles and I told

him everything about the letter and my father so

we drink and talk and drink and talk until

I don't remember what time in the night.

All finished in a bed and that man I was with was

married for one year and he had no children yet

and I knew all about that. After me have done this

he saw that I was still a virgin he told me Diana

don't tell me I was your first man? I said yes, it's

the first time I been doing that.

So, after this I called the La Plante taxi and I told

Julian bring me home, that's what he did. And on

Monday I went to my job I saw my man of one

night and time pass until after Christmas holiday

I start to get sick every morning and I go see my

Doctor he told me you are pregnant.

I said how come I did that once only and you tell

me that I'm pregnant he said yes two months.

I give him my last date I said which month will

I have my baby? He said in August between the

10th and the 17th I was horrified. So, time goes

by and my uniform began to be too tight every two

weeks I had to take a bigger size so I give my

notice to the hospital where I was working.

I quit my job I went to Mariette La Fortune's

home in Lachine it was not very far from Perrot

Island. I went there with Julian La Plante who

didn't know anything about my pregnancy

because I never been in bed with him at all.

He was only a good friend but when I told that to Mariette and Gerald who was involved at that time they thought my baby was Julian's but they didn't say anything to me about it and when I had my baby (you) on August 15th Gerald told Mariette I'm going to see that Julian La Plante for what he made to my sister. Mariette told me the day after so I couldn't say no it wasn't him, because Gerald will ask me the real man who was that man and so on. I didn't want to break his marriage of that man even if he has broken mine but I continue to say it was Julian La Plante. But he knows and I know damn well it wasn't him. When Gerald talked to Julian Gerald was very furious. But that poor man said "No, it's not my baby". I didn't even talk to Julian about my pregnancy! Even the real, your real father doesn't know about my pregnancy because it wasn't his fault it wasn't my fault it was just an adventure of a night that's all.

But I pay the price for it and it costs me my dear

baby, because I was too sick to take care of him,

no money no husband. But I said to Gerald my

brother who helped me so much during all that

hard time, if there is a God I swear before I die,

I will be able to see my baby again. Gerald has

never known who your father's name was.

You are the first and the principal person that

today I will tell you his name!

It was RENE CHEVRIER and now stop your

research and forget Julian La Plante.

I beg you to forgive my false please. This is all the

story of your and my life since Nov. 4th, 1955

Your Mother Diane Cbiasson Thank you for

reading this letter."

I gave the letter to Rick to read. We sat in his car in

silence. We drove back to Rick's home and I showed

the letter to his wife Fran. She said there is only one

thing I could do, was call the private investigator to

tell him what had happened.

Maybe he could find information on this Rene

Chevrier. I went into their backyard to play with

their sons Matthew and Christopher.

I had to think this over. I would leave the next day

for Germany. Time was running out. I came back

into Rick's house to call the private investigator.

He told me he would check it out and call me back

as soon as possible. I received his call the next day.

Rene had apparently worked at the hospital back

then but went to work for the electric company as

his real career. The investigator informed me he

was sorry to say Rene Chevrier had died!

Other Chevrier's were still working at that hospital.

Maybe I could call them from Germany to see if

one of them would send me a photo.

I called Diane to say goodbye to her over the

phone. I told her I needed some time to digest it all.

I didn't tell her that Rene had died. I was waiting at

the airport in Montreal and called home to

Germany. My roommate Gerhard Telger answered

the phone and asked, "Are you okay you sound

funny?"

I burst into tears and I could hardly speak. I told

him I had waited too long to find my father; he was

dead. I composed myself and called Julian La

Plante one last time. His wife answered the phone.

She said he really didn't want to talk to me again.

I asked her to tell Julian that he was right all along.

I had finally found out the truth and I apologized to

them on behalf of my family. I said that I hoped

I hadn't caused them any problems. I ended the

conversation by saying, "Thank you and may God

bless you." Mrs. LaPlante was very kind and

wished me a safe flight home! I felt badly I had

bothered them. Had I never called him in the first

place, I would have gone to my grave thinking

Julian La Plante was my father. After all these years

I had at least cleared his name. The truth had finally

come out after 42 years! Or at least I thought that it

had.

THE CHEVRIER BROTHERS   CHAPTER 10

A few days after I came home, I decided to call the
hospital. I asked to speak to Mr. Chevrier. A woman
at the other end said, "One moment please."
Suddenly, a young voice on the phone said hello to
me. I asked "Is this Mr. Chevrier." He said "Yes, this
is Jerry Chevrier. Who is this?" I told him who I
was. I explained I had every reason to believe we
were related. I wondered if he could send me a
picture of Rene Chevrier. He told me that was his
Uncle and he was his Godchild. Rene and his wife
had never had children and Jerry was like a son to
Rene. I sensed he was upset about my call. He didn't
want to hear something like this about an Uncle he
had loved so much. I asked him what Rene had died
of. He told me it had been lung cancer.
I said, "Can I have a picture of Rene?" I just wanted
to see what he had looked like. His response was,
"Let me talk to my father about this first." He told me
to call back in two days, as he had the next day off.

I agreed and looked forward to our next

conversation. Two days later I called the hospital

again. I spoke to Jerry. He said to me right away,

"Please call my father." and gave me his phone

number. I dialed the number immediately.

A man answered and I introduced myself. He knew

who I was and why I had called. For the next five

minutes, I just listened to what he had to say, it was

unbelievable. He told me I had found the wrong

Rene Chevrier. There was another Rene who had

worked at the hospital. He continued to say that the

one I was looking for, was still alive and had just

retired. Apparently, Rene had worked in the kitchen

as a cook. His brother Rene had worked in the

maintenance department only briefly, until he took a

permanent job with the electric company.

He told me, he knew the other Rene even though they

were not related. My father was recently divorced

and lived with his sister Marie. He gave me his

address and phone number. I told him I couldn't have

thanked him enough for his help. He wished me

good luck!

I hung up the phone completely confused. Was it possible my father was still alive? Could there really be two Rene Chevriers? I called the private investigator and asked him to check this possibility. Meanwhile, I called Diane. She was very happy to hear from me. I asked her, "What was Rene's job at the hospital when you were there?". Her response was; "He had worked in the kitchen. Why do you ask me this question?". I told her I just needed to know and I would call her back in a few days. The next day I received a call from the private investigator. Yes, there was a second Rene Chevrier. He apologized to me for his oversight. He then told me, I would make a good private investigator myself. I informed him that I already had obtained the second Rene's address and phone number. I couldn't believe it my father was still alive! What were the chances of that? I thought about what I would say to Rene when I called him. But when he answered the phone, I lost all of my thoughts. I cleared my throat and told him my name.

I asked if he remembered a girl from the 1950's by

the name of Diana Cbiasson from St. Anne of

Bellevue Hospital. He said. "No" "I don't." I told him

why I had called. He became really quiet on the

phone, you could have heard a pin drop. Then he said

to me, "Well, what do you want. Money?" I couldn't

help but laugh, because I knew he was nervous and

worried all at once. I told him I had my own money

and didn't want any of his. He asked again "Well,

then what do you want?" I told him I would like the

opportunity to meet him in person, someday.

I asked if he would mail me a picture of himself.

I told him I planned on coming to Montreal again in

April of 1999 for my sister Colette's birthday.

He agreed to send me a picture, which he did do.

Before I came to Montreal, I should call him so that

we could meet one another. I sat in my office and

thought, "This guy doesn't want any trouble from

me." I wasn't out to cause him trouble.

I just wanted to meet him. He told me his birthday

was also in August and that he was born on

August 6, 1925.

I thought my mother is a Leo, my father is a Leo and so am I. He told me he had three children, two boys and a girl. He was recently divorced after 40 years of marriage. I asked him, "Why get divorced after 40 years?" He responded by saying it was because he was afraid of flying over the ocean. He would not go to Europe with his wife for their 40th wedding anniversary. So, she left him. He asked me several questions about how I found Diane. He also wanted to know if l was married and had any children?
I responded I have no biological children and I wasn't married. I decided not to mention to him I was gay! The conversation was pleasant, though I could tell he was rather nervous. I hung up the phone and thought, "He's alright and I have three more siblings on his side of the family."

April 9, 1999

I flew to Montreal to meet my biological father.
I had timed it around my sister Colette's birthday.
I stayed at the Sheraton Hotel in Laval, located
across the street from a huge shopping mall.

I called Rene and we agreed to meet on April 10th.
in the lobby of the hotel. Afterwards, we would go
for lunch at the mall. Renee Monette's
grandchildren, Mia, Renee, Richard and Andre
came over to see me. They wanted to go out
dancing, but I was too nervous about meeting Rene
the next day, to go out. Renee Monette's family
was there once again offering me their well wishes
and support. It is true that the apple doesn't fall far
from the tree. April 10, 1999

After what happened during dinner in Detroit
seven years before, I also celebrate April 10th as my
birthday. I was finally going to meet my
biological father on my seventh birthday. I waited
in the lobby of the Sheraton Hotel and Rene
Chevrier walked in right on time. He had
brought his younger brother Yvan with him for
moral support and for physical protection just in
case he would need it. I had exactly the same eyes
as his brother. I could tell by looking at Rene, we
were related. I had his arms and his hands.

He had this golden glow on the top of his hair just like mine does, when exposed to the sun. By the way they looked at each other they knew we were related. Rene was about five-foot eight or so. I am a little over six feet, I thought, "Thank God I have my grandfather's height on Diane's side of the family." He started by saying that he couldn't recall the encounter with my mother years ago at all. I asked him, "Well, how many girls did you sleep with over the years?" He asked me again if l wanted something from him? I said, "No, not really. Just tell me about your family health. How old are my brothers and sister?" He said cancer seemed to run in his family but not until in their 80's. He told me his older sister he was living with was sick. He had some health issues himself. I asked him what was wrong with him. He replied that it was his liver. We talked about his three children. Roseanne was his first, then came Robert. In his forties he and his wife had another baby, which they named Richard.

"Richard" I said, I could hardly believe I had a second brother named Richard, how bizarre! Rene said, "Yeah, can you believe all of my children's names start with the letter R. Just like mine. And so, does yours." Rene had a big smile on his face. I told him I was the only person in my family whose name started with the letter R. Most of my relatives had names that started with the letter T. We decided to go across the street to have lunch. The name of the restaurant was 'Baton Rouge'. I thought it fitting, because translated it means the red bat or in slang a big red hard one! It was so appropriate, but not intended or planned. We all laughed when we looked up at the name of the restaurant. Maybe it was the icebreaker we all needed. Yvan was very nice to me. I ordered a beer and asked Rene if he would have one as well. Yvan said, "Well, I don't think one will hurt you. If there was ever a day for you to have a drink, this is it"! I asked Rene, "You don't drink?" He replied, "I am not supposed to, because of my liver." We talked about my life in California.

I told him I had little parts in some movies.

He wanted to see 'Top Gun' again to look for me.
I told him to look fast as I am only in it for about
ten seconds. He seemed impressed that one of his
offspring had made it into movies. Then he asked
me something I never expected, "Do you want to
have my last name?" I was really surprised that he
asked me this question. It was a nice gesture, but
I responded, "No thanks, I am Tom Geiger's son!"
I never felt prouder in my life to say those words.
I had always been proud to be Tom Geiger's son,
but I had never said it with such assurance before.
Rene went to the restroom and Yvan just looked at
me and smiled. Then he said to me,
"Look give me your telephone number. When my
brother dies, I will call you to meet your other
brothers and sister." I agreed with him that was a
good idea. Yvan asked me if l had spent time with
my mother's family. I said,
"Yes, we are all having a big family brunch
tomorrow at the Sheraton Hotel." I told Yvan that
Diane's family was really nice.

They all loved me like I had been in their family
forever. When Rene came back to the table,
I asked him about his divorce.

He said that his marriage had its ups and downs.
When he refused to fly to Europe with his wife,
she told him she had put up with enough over the
years. If he did not get on that plane with her, on
returning she would leave him. Rene said that he
had not believed her, but she did it! His children
were furious he had not gone to Paris.

He didn't go into much more detail other than his
kids were just finally speaking to him again, after
all that had happened. If they would find out about
me, he was afraid how they would react. He said,
"Can you do an old man a favor? Let me live the
few remaining years I have in harmony with my
kids." They had barely forgiven him for not
going on the trip with their mother. This would
be too much for them. It would surely ruin what
time he had left with them. His son Robert had a
son and he showed me his picture. He also showed
me one of his daughter Roseanne.

Since I was not out to ruin this man's life, I agreed

I would stay away from his children for as long

as possible. I told him they would hate him for

not telling them before, when they found out.

He responded by saying, "Better for them to hate

me after I am gone, instead of these last few years."

I trusted my Uncle Yvan to call me when my

father had died. We took a couple of photos of

each other together in the parking lot.

I called him around Christmas and on his birthdays

ever since. He has always been nice to me on the

phone and always asks when I will come to

Montreal again. "Hopefully next Spring."

I always say. He always tells me to call him to go

to lunch again. I think he liked me.

We both respected each other's position in this

delicate matter. I went back to my hotel room to

call my Dad. He was on his boat in Florida

however, so I couldn't reach him.

I really needed to talk to him to tell him how much

I loved him and that I was glad to be HIS son.

I then called my friend Marta Stiles in California
and told her how it had gone with Rene and it
certainly helped calm my nerves. I really needed to
talk to someone close to my heart. What an
unforgettable day this had been. I remember saying
to Marta that Rene had these incredible blues eyes
just like she did! April 11, 1999

The next day I had a wonderful Sunday brunch
with my mother's family. I told Diane about my
meeting with Rene. She seemed surprised to hear
he was divorced after 40 years of marriage. She
asked me if l would call his children.

I said, "Probably not until Rene is dead!"

I looked at all my relatives in the banquet room
I was lucky I had finally put all the missing pieces
together. My parents were both still alive and
I had met them. At that moment I realized
I had ten siblings now. My brother Tom and sister
Gigi, who I grew up with. Diane's five children
Ronald, Alain, Richard, Colette and Andre.

And Rene's three kids Roseanne, Robert and

Richard. It was funny, growing up I had always

wanted ten siblings. Now I had them! Having two

brothers named Richard still seems odd to me.

April 12, 1999 On my sister Colette's 32nd

birthday we took a Limo all over Montreal.

Of course, we went up to St. Joseph's Cathedral

to light two candles for Mary. We had a delicious

lunch at a beautiful restaurant located on an

island called 'Helene DeChamplain'.

The restaurant owner even let me play the piano

for my sister, while we were there. It was a

beautiful grand piano. The owner had bought it,

because many famous people had used it for their

performances. The sound that came out of this

piano was perfect! I was really thrilled the owner

let me play it for Colette. It was even more of a

delight, because she had never seen me play the

piano before. She had only heard me play on the

telephone, so it was really great she could see me

play.

My sister and I told the limo driver we were

brother and sister. We were so excited to spend

her birthday together, because I had been

adopted. I told him what had happened.

Our driver told us he had come from the same

orphanage as me but he was never adopted.

He was released early by enlisting in the military.

We compared childhood stories on the way to the

airport. His story at the Orphanage was very sad.

He told me that my story was unbelievable and

that I should write a book about it because an

Angel had looked out for me. I thought about

what the limo driver had said to me and how

lucky I was to have not stayed in that orphanage!

On the long flight back home to Europe, I started

to write my story.

THE GERMAN COUPLE   CHAPTER 11

In Spring of 2004 I had recently opened a small

clothing store in Germany. I was incredibly busy

with this new project. Suddenly, my cell phone rang.

I answered the phone, "Geiger", as I usually do.

A man's voice asked me if I was Richard Geiger,

whose father was from the Montreal Chevrier's.

I responded by asking how he knew this information.

The man said that he was a friend of the Chevrier's.

He and his wife wanted to come to my town to speak

to me. I told him about my new business.

He would have to meet me there, because I was never

at home during the day. He said he and his wife

would see me in a few days. I thought at first it was

nice that they wanted to meet me. Then I started to

think about it and wondered what it was they wanted

to talk to me about. A few days later,

I noticed an older looking couple walking towards

the store.

Since my store was geared towards 13 to 30-year

ages, I knew this was the couple that had called me.

They walked into the store and looked at me.

They said, "You must be Richard, because you

certainly look like one of your brothers."

I said to them I had never met any of my half-

siblings on my father's side. Then they said

something I had never expected.

They came to tell me my biological father had died!

I said, "When did he die?" They said he had died in

December 2002. They felt I ought to know the truth.

I told them they were confused. I had just spoken to

my father over Christmas of 2003. How could Rene

be dead for more than a year? They responded

Gerard was my real father and not Rene.

Then they handed me a newspaper clipping showing

Gerard's death announcement.

They knew more about my true paternity than I did.

They insisted it was important for me to know the

truth. My real father was Gerard Chevrier, Rene's

younger brother. I couldn't believe what these two

people were saying.

They said not to worry, because Yvan Chevrier
would say he had been my father so the Chevrier's
would not forget me. I was totally shocked by what
I had heard! I responded offensively; stating they
didn't have a clue what they were saying! Rene didn't
want his children to know about me, until he was
dead. The story they had been told was obviously a
cover up. They immediately responded it was not
Rene's son that I looked like, but Gerard's son
Christian Chevrier. They handed me a Chevrier
business card from Canada. They could tell I still
didn't believe what they had said.

I was so upset about their visit, that I still don't
remember their names. That's why I always refer to
them as the German couple! My store had gotten
quite busy, so I used my waiting customers as an
excuse to basically ask them to leave the store.

They repeated Gerard Chevrier was my real father.
If l checked out their story, I would find out it was
true. After they left my store, I pushed it out of my
mind until I arrived home that night and discussed it
with my family.

Everyone said, "Do you think they are right and you were misled?" I thought about the possibility of two brothers somehow taking advantage of a drunk 19 - year old girl who was in the wrong place at the wrong time. Rene would want to protect his brother and himself from embarrassment if this was true.

I needed to ask Diane more about that night, so I called her. I didn't tell her what the German couple had told me. I asked her to relive that night. She said she had been so drunk, she passed out. She had really forgotten most of the night, until she woke up in the morning with Rene. She wanted to know why I asked. I told her I needed to know whether she remembered that night at all. I needed to know what had happened. The way she responded, implied she didn't really want to remember all of it. I let it go for a few more months. Then I decided to call Rene Chevrier to wish him a happy birthday.

I told him that I did not appreciate friends of his family coming into my store with such nonsense. Rene responded by saying he "didn't want to talk about that night ever again."

He told me to forget about it. I said I couldn't just

forget. I would call his son Robert after Rene's

birthday in August. I allowed him the space of time

to talk to his oldest son Robert first. Perhaps I would

find out if Rene was my father that way.

I sensed he wasn't happy with our telephone

conversation. I felt he was hiding something from

me. Could it be possible that his brother had been

involved with my mother that night too?

If this was true, no wonder Rene didn't want to talk

about that night with my mother. I called my Uncle

Yvan and someone named Sylvie Chevrier answered

the business line. I introduced myself, and told her

what had happened to me. I admitted I had been very

upset about a visit I received from a German couple

I didn't mention to her the German couple had

claimed Gerard Chevrier was my father, just that

they insisted on discussing my paternity.

I asked her not to tell Rene's children about our

conversation until I had spoken to Robert myself.

I told her I had spoken to Therese Chevrier.

She responded by saying that Therese was both her

Aunt and God-mother. I said I was coming to

Montreal in October. I would try to resolve this

matter at that time. Sylvie was very quiet on the

phone, but she listened politely to what I had to say.

I hung up the phone, wondering whether she was my

half-sister or my cousin? Either way, I had to know

the truth and Rene needed to help me. I didn't believe

what the German couple had told me. Somehow,

I managed to bury what they had said to me deep in

my head. I thought they were completely wrong and

misinformed. I waited until Rene had turned eighty

years old in August 2005 to call his son.

Robert immediately said he had spoken to his father

about my phone call. His father had said there was a

man going around claiming to be his son.

Rene was not sure that this was true. Robert

suggested we do a DNA test. I completely agreed

with him that this was the best way to handle this

delicate matter. We agreed I'd make the

arrangements to have the test done when I would

come to Montreal.

I planned to go to my brother Richard's 40th birthday in late October in just a few months from then.

I thanked Robert for his time. Later I received an e-mail from both his sister and brother. I looked a little like his younger brother Richard.

I could see a family resemblance. I called the most reputable testing site I could find in Montreal, PRO-ADN Diagnostic. The company had a very good reputation. They required both parties to sign release and consent forms for the type of DNA testing that needed to be done and valid photo identification. On the day of the test they would also make pictures of the test-subjects involved.

I made the appointment for October 27, 2005 and wrote the following letter to Robert.

August 29, 2005

"Dear Robert, it was a pleasure to finally have the chance to speak with you for the first time. Even though under the circumstances I still want you to know that I never have asked for anything from the Chevrier's nor will I ever ask for anything from any of you except for the chance to meet you and Roseanne and Richard. Meeting all of you would be the greatest thing you could do for me. I have checked around regarding your request about the DNA testing and this is the best place that we can go to in Montreal. It will show that Rene is my father and it can show that you are my half-brother. The costs are quite high so what if we split the costs and if it comes back not true then I will pay for all of it! I truly believe that my natural mother Diana is being honest about all of this. She simply states that she has only slept with two men in her entire life. Rene Chevrier on November 4, 1955 and then only her husband who she married in 1959. She tried to keep this a secret for many years about what happened one night between her and Rene.

However, since I am a product of that one-time experience, I feel that I had the right to meet all of my brothers and sisters. I have ten totaled. My natural mother has five other children all younger than me with her husband (four boys and one girl) then the Geiger's who adopted me through the Catholic Church have three children including me. So just like you I was raised with one brother and one sister. As I told you over the telephone, I have a wonderful life and only want the chance to meet all of you. The DNA test will confirm what is true. I will call you a few days before I fly to Montreal so we can meet and do the DNA testing first. Either you or Rene can do the test. Of course, it would be nice of Rene to do it himself but you being my half-brother will show that to be true. I don't want to argue over this DNA testing with Rene he is very sick and eighty years old. I did give him the extra time that he wanted to have with all of you. Remember you three children mean the world to him. YOU ARE HIS WORLD!

I have enclosed in French the information regarding

the place we can have the DNA testing done on

October 27th would be a good day for me to do this

because I will fly on the 26th of October and my

brother's 40th birthday party is on Saturday the 29th.

I do want to spend as much time with Diana's family

as possible and I plan to fly back to Europe on the

31st of October. So, for us to do this DNA testing the

27th or 28th of October would be the easiest for me.

I would love to have the chance to have lunch with

all three of you but only if Richard and Roseanne

are open to the idea. Also, if your Aunt Therese

wants to come for lunch she is invited as my guest

because as I told you she was the only one who ever

called and apologized on behalf of the Chevrier's.

She didn't need to do that but when she did,

I was very happy to know that someone from your

family cared at all! I have never met her and would

like to meet her since she always wanted to meet me.

I look forward to meeting you Robert. Sincerely,

Richard. A few days after sending that letter

I received a phone call from my Mom in Ohio.

She was crying. She told me that my Aunt Laurie was

dying of a rare lung disease. I had to come home

quickly. Laurie was younger than me.

She had married my Uncle Tim more than twenty

years ago. The next day I flew to Toledo, but Laurie

died while I was on the airplane. At Laurie's funeral

I noticed my Mom didn't look well. I thought it was

the stress of Laurie's death. Still, I asked my Mom if

she was okay? She said, "Not so good, really"

and described her symptoms. I looked at her and

said, "Mom, you have lymphoma!"

"No, I don't!" she replied, "Mom you just described

every symptom of lymphoma." I felt her neck on the

way home and found a swollen lymph node.

I called my sister that night. I told her I would leave

for Germany the next morning. She had to make sure

Mom went to her doctor. After landing back in

Germany my sister called me to say she had felt

some swollen lymph nodes around Mom's neck too.

My sister said, "I don't have a good feeling about

this!" My sister took our Mom to the doctor the next

day.

She was indeed diagnosed with non-Hodgkin's disease. Everything changed at that moment, no one was more important than my Mom. I called the Chevrier's and cancelled the DNA test until my Mother would have finished her Chemotherapy treatments. We waited for weeks to find out if the treatments were working or hurting her more. After a month or so had past, we were all delighted to find out my Mom results were very positive. Everyone in our family came for a huge, delicious Thanksgiving dinner at her home. I stayed with my Mom for several weeks. We had long wonderful talks about our lives together. She was completely at peace with her world. Her connection to God was a strong as ever! The effects of the chemotherapy treatments were too much for her body to handle and she went into a coma. My Mom passed away February 10, 2006. I think of her every day and thank God for choosing her as my Mother. After dealing with her funeral and personal belongings, I called Robert Chevrier. We rescheduled our DNA appointments for April 25th 2006 at 11:00 a.m.

The DNA Results   Chapter 12

I arrived in Montreal on the 24th of April.

Naturally, I went out to dinner with Rick, Fran

and their children. We ate at an Italian restaurant

in Laval and watched a hockey game on a big

screen T.V. It was great having fun with

longtime friends and seeing how much their kids

had grown up. I called my sister Colette before

I went to sleep. She offered to go with me to take

the DNA test. Since Rene probably wouldn't

come alone, I would have someone with me.

I agreed with her. Her home was on the way to

PRO-ADN, so I picked her up along the way.

We arrived at 10:50 a.m. Rene was walking in

the parking lot next to the clinic with two other

men. I said to Colette, "That must be Robert,

because he looks younger than me."

The other man looked like an older brother of

Rene's. They didn't see us until we walked into

the building.

My heart raced as I shook Rene's hand.

Rene looked a bit different than I recalled.

Robert introduced a man named Real to us.

He was Rene's brother. We signed release forms

and showed I.D. The procedure consisted of a

quick swabbing of a stick inside our mouths.

The technician took a photo of me directly

afterwards. All five of us spoke briefly in the

walkway. Then we took a few photos.

The clinic would send out the analysis of the

paternity test by certified letter. We should

expect it to take three to four weeks before being

mailed out to us. The Chevriers said they had no

time for lunch. We would talk after receiving the

results. I thanked Rene for coming in himself.

Then I spoke to his brother Real.

He gave me his telephone number and asked to

give it to my mother. They lived close to one

another and he wanted to talk to her. Real said

I should call him sometime too. I spent the rest

of my time in Montreal with Diane and her

family.

I was there for only three days, so we spent

almost every hour together.

Waiting for the DNA results was a little nerve

racking, but I had waited longer than this for

information regarding my adoption. I flew back

home and waited for my certified letter to arrive.

It wasn't until almost the end of May that the

letter arrived in Germany. With my friend

Michel next to me I slowly opened it. I couldn't

believe my eyes, Rene Chevrier was not my

biological father! The results stated, there was

zero percent chance he was my biological father.

I was stunned! For over seven years

I had thought this man was my father.

Now I found out that he wasn't. This was

shocking to me, to say the least. I immediately

called Diane and told her about the results. Diane

couldn't believe it either, she remembered him.

I told Diane to think about that night again.

From the moment she got out of the taxi to go

into the hotel. She said, "I remember looking

around the room.

Just a few people were there and I ordered a

drink. Then I saw Rene Chevrier. Said hello and

sat with him." I asked Diane, "Did anyone else

come to the table or have a drink with you?"

She said "Well, yes. His brother came in later

and had a drink." I asked, "Do you remember his

name?". Diane said, "No, but he was closer to

my age than to Rene's." I told Diane about the

German couple that had come into my store back

in 2004. She started to talk about that night. She

realized the second time she had sex that night,

may not have been with Rene again but with his

brother. Diane remembered the second time

taking place. She always thought it had been

Rene doing it to her again. She said she really

couldn't remember that night, that she's buried it

emotionally somehow. She did remember having

sex twice, but she always thought it had just been

with Rene. It was possible his brother had taken

advantage of the situation. Diane had been so

drunk, she blacked out in the middle of the night.

She was very upset on the phone and began to cry. Her husband Harvey got upset by the idea that two brothers had taken advantage of a drunk, teenage girl. I told Diane I would call Gerard Chevrier's children. I would explain the situation to them; surely one of Gerard's sons would help me. I promised Diane I would find out the truth somehow. I calmed Diane and her husband down. I reminded Harvey all of this had happened way before he even knew my mother. He agreed with me. I knew Diane had not made up her story about Rene and that night. She had truly blocked out the part about the second man in the bedroom. Rene thought that he was my father, because there was a good chance that he was. I called the DNA clinic to ask if they could tell Rene was my Uncle. They stated that Rene and I had not done that type of testing.

Only additional testing could establish any other family relation than paternity. I asked, "Could we do this kind of testing now?"

They said, "Only if both parties agree to sign a release form for these extra tests." I called Real Chevrier to ask him what he thought about the chance of his other brother Gerard being my father. Real said that Rene was very mad at him for speaking to me. Furthermore, Rene said his friend Phillippe Chevrier had been with him that night, so Phillippe must be my father. "Why is Rene now suddenly willing to talk?" I said to Real, "Do you believe that story from Rene?" Real said it was what his brother told him to say. Real stated that he had spoken with Diane she told him I was gay. He wanted me to know that he was also gay and never slept with a woman. I told him I had dated both sexes but realized that I was gay. We laughed for a moment about the possibility of a gay gene in the Chevrier family. I said I was going to ask Robert for help. If he wouldn't help me, I would ask one of Gerard's sons. I told Real, if the DNA didn't match Gerard's family then I would believe Rene's story about Phillippe.

I wrote Robert the following letter dated

June 25, 2006

"Dear Robert, I hope that you and your family
are enjoying the summer.

I tried to call you but was unsuccessful in
reaching you in person. So, I decided to write you
this letter to explain where I am at with all of this
information. I have been told by different people
during this whole ordeal that my true father is
Gerald Chevrier and that the DNA test would
show if that is true because they can run another
test to see if your father Rene is my Uncle and
now some claim that it is Phillipe Chevrier.
We can find out with the DNA we have given
them is a fact or not a fact that it can't be Gerald
and that the story now about Philippe Chevrier
has to be true and this leaves your family
completely unrelated to me. I do feel that there is
a possibility it is true about your Uncle Gerald
because of what the German couple who are
friends of your family told me in 2004 after
Gerald had died.

I didn't believe them because at the time I always thought it was Rene but now the DNA test shows that he isn't but with the DNA they have on file they can run another kind of test ruling out any relation what so ever. Perhaps we do find out that Rene is indeed my Uncle and that you're my cousin. I think that Sylvie Chevrier and her brothers would like to know 100% if this is true or not about their father? Ever since the German couple told me that Gerald was my real father this additional testing would find out once and for all. If it comes back no relation then we have the answers for myself and also for Gerald's children too! If it comes back true then you and I are cousins. It was sad enough to lose you as a brother...so cousins would be nice. I think running the extra test is worth doing to see if we are related in any way. The DNA place is mailing out a form for you or your father to sign to run the additional testing with the DNA they have already.

Rene did not have to go back there again. Just signing the form is enough.

I said I will gladly pay for the costs and you will receive your own copy just like the last time.

I should have run both test when we were there but I did not think about a second guy until after we did the testing. I did not even give any thought to what the Germans had told me back in 2004 until after I thought there could be a second man involved that night. "Robert, I hope that you will help me resolve this last issue of being related or not being related, I must say that I do have some resemblance to the Chevrier family and I hope that you speak with Sylvie Chevrier and her brothers and decide what is best for all of us to do. If Rene does not want the other test run then perhaps one of Gerald's sons would be willing to do so. The easiest thing for us to do is to run a further test on the DNA we already gave to them.

I am still blown away that Rene is not my father

and I would like this last test done to rule out

this other rumour about your uncle Gerald.

Robert, you cannot imagine how all of this feels.

Please let me know what you decide to do. I have

sent in my consent form already to the DNA

place and they are sending you one to send back

to them. Thanks, Robert, for handling this

delicate matter so nicely, I appreciate your help.

Sincerely, Richard."

When I got no response to my letter,

I called Robert. He told me his father wouldn't

sign any more forms. Then he said his father had

said that a friend of his had been there that night

with my mother and Rene, named Philippe

Chevrier. They were not related and I must be

Phillippe's son. I didn't believe what Rene said

about what happened that night. I told Robert

I was more determined now than ever to find out

if Gerard was my biological father. Robert

responded by saying, "What are you going to do?

Go around and ask every Chevrier for their

DNA?" I said, "No, just Gerard Chevrier's sons."

Maybe one of them will help me find out the

truth. I knew what Robert had meant with his

remark, but he couldn't understand how it felt to

be this close to the truth. I wasn't about to stop

from finding the answer. I suppose the letter

I wrote him was a bit confusing. I misspelled

Sylvie's and Gerard's name throughout the entire

letter. I was really desperate for Robert to help

me but he decided against further assistance.

I waited until July to call Sylvie Chevrier.

I asked her if she had heard about the DNA

results from Robert or Rene. She said she had

heard the results had been negative. I reminded

her I had called her about the German couple in

2004. Sylvie stated that she remembered.

I told her they had said that her father Gerard,

was also my biological father! I explained that

I needed one of her brothers to go to PRO-ADN

in Montreal to do a DNA test for me to prove or

disprove what the Germans told me.

Sylvie waited a moment before she asked one of her brothers in the background to do a DNA test. His response was, "No." Her brother Stephane got on the phone. He said he would do the test for me. We spoke about it briefly. Both of us wanted to know if what the German couple had said, or what Rene Chevrier had said about his friend Phillippe, was true. I felt more inclined to believe the German couple, what would they gain by saying it was Gerard? Rene however, had not been forthcoming about anything that happened that night with Diane.

He wanted to protect his younger brother's family of the embarrassment. I called the DNA clinic to ask what was required for Stephane to take the test for half-siblings? They informed me it would work best if my mother came in, so they could compare her numbers to mine.

The remaining numbers would then have to come from the paternal side of my genetic make-up. I called Diane and asked her to go into the DNA clinic.

At first, Diane didn't want to go into a clinic.

Then she agreed and Colette took her on July 18,

2006. Without her help the rest of the test

wouldn't be so easy. Fortunately,

for me the male DNA doesn't change one

generation to another. My mother's DNA was

compared to mine. The matching numbers were

deleted from my genetic make-up. The

remaining numbers were male DNA only.

Comparing these to Stephane's DNA numbers

would tell us the truth. My fiftieth birthday was

coming up. I had hoped to have this resolved by

then. No such luck! I waited until mid-

September before calling the Chevrier's to ask if

Stephane was still willing to do the test. Sylvie

answered the phone. She said they had all talked

about the DNA test the other day. She confirmed

Stephane would still go in. She explained he had

been too busy with work to go.

On September 21, 2006

Stephane went into the clinic and submitted his
DNA for comparison.

Saturday November 11, 2006

I will never forget. I was staying at the Grand
Hyatt in Berlin with out of town friends.

My cell phone rang. It was Michel calling me
from our home. He said, "Are you sitting down?"

I responded, "Yes, why?"

Michel said my DNA results had come in. He
signed for them and wanted to open it and read
me the results. He read, "Based on the analysis of
the above-mentioned genetic markers, Mr.
Stephane Chevrier cannot be excluded as
biologic half-sibling of Mr. Richard J. Geiger.
There are strong biologic indicators (combined
parentage index of 119) that Mr.Stephane
Chevrier is half-sibling of Mr. Richard J. Geiger.
The parentage probability is 99,17%. Analysis
completed on Nov 3rd 2006."

I started to yell and laugh on the phone. Neither
one of us could believe it.

The German couple had been right all along; my father was Gerard! They tried so hard to tell me the truth back in 2004. If only I could apologize to the German couple for not believing them. Now, I have eleven siblings; Tom, Gigi, Ronald, Alain, Richard, Colette, Andre, Sylvie, Gilbert, Christian and Stephane. Gerard had four children with his wife. At least there is only one brother named Richard instead of two, which makes it a little easier. Finally, I had the answer to who my biological father was. Gerard Chevrier was born on December 2, 1935 and died December 22, 2002. I called Diane immediately. She said she still couldn't believe it was his brother Gerard not Rene. "DNA never lies!" I said back to her.

I was very happy about the DNA results. Diane was relieved that after all these years both of us had finally found out the entire truth.

I realized it was November 2006, thirty years before I had started my claim with the Canadian Courts in November 1976.

Thirty years had pass bye and I finally had all the

answers to my adoption. I called Stephane and

his sister Sylvie answered the work phone.

I ask for him, but he wasn't there. I told her I had

received my results. I was rather surprised, but

relieved my search was over. She said Stephane

had not picked up his letter from the post office

yet. I excused myself for thinking they would

have already known the results. I could tell she

was very surprised. I said I would call again to

speak to Stephane to thank him for helping me

find out the truth. I sent him a gift from the

United States with a card saying, "Thank you for

doing right by me!" Eventually Stephane and

I spoke on the phone. We were both surprised by

the DNA results. We made plans to meet each

other in Spring, on my visit to Montreal.

I feel very blessed to know the truth. The

question, "Why I was given up for adoption?"

was answered. I am at peace with all of it!

Of course, finding out the truth took some work

and a great deal of time.

There are lessons to learn here. One; watch how much you drink. It can impair your better judgement and cause lots of trouble. Two, if you really want an answer to a question, keep searching, there's always an answer! Don't ever give up hope! The day will come that you find the answers to those questions. Three, I am happy that I found out the truth, even if the truth was not pleasant! I also regret not believing in the German couple. They tried so hard to tell me the truth. Many people helped me along the way in my search for my natural parents. This couple was one of them; thank you wherever you are! I should have been more open-minded about what they tried to say to me. This experience has taught me a very valuable lesson. Some things are worth fighting for, even if it takes thirty years to reach the goal. I plan on flying to Montreal in Spring. I am very much looking forward to meeting my four half siblings on the Chevrier side. We planned to meet for dinner at the W. Hotel.

I met all my siblings on the Chevrier side except Stephane, whose wife was having a baby around that time. Christian Chevrier and I did look quite a bit alike just like the German couple said.

The Chevrier siblings were very nice people and we had a lovely dinner together. I have never seen them again. A few years later, I was informed of Rene's passing by Diane in Canada. I realized after Rene died and looking at his picture in his obituary in the paper that he was not who I met in Montreal back in 1999. That is why he looked different to me at the DNA place. His eyes did not look as blue as they did in Laval. I realized that it was actually Gerard who had showed up that day with his brother Yvan. They led me to believe that he was Rene because that is who I thought I would be meeting. I have a photographic memory and I can clearly see the face of Gerard as the man that I met in Laval. As I looked at both Rene's and Gerard's Obituary pictures it was definitely Gerard that I met that day in 1999 with his brother Yvan.

So, it turns out that I did really meet my biological father once before he died. It was not Rene who met me in Laval that day but Gerard himself with his brother Yvan! He never did say his first name and I addressed him as Mr. Chevrier. So, I was misled by the Chevriers myself! I can understand why Gerard did what he did that day in Laval making me think he was Rene. To protect his family as long as he could before his death. Gerard did keep his word and finally let the truth out via the German couple, carefully waiting to let me know until his passing before I found out the complete truth on who made me with Diane! The DNA results confirmed the Germans story.

I feel very blessed to have found the answers to my questions regarding my adoption. I never gave up hope that I would find out the truth through my persistence. I knew there was an answer waiting to be found. I hold no grudges against Rene, Gerard or Diane, for what happened between them back in 1955. How Diane reacted to my coming into this world was up to her. I am sure being a teenager and being Catholic in the mid 1950's it was terrifying to her. I love being a Geiger and the Geiger's wanted children. I would not have wanted any other parents in the world than the two God had picked for me Thomas and Therese Geiger.

I just wanted to know the truth about whomever I came from and what my biological family's roots were. Both the Chiasson and Chevrier families are good decent people, I am happy that I met my biological families. When you have goals to reach never give up, keep trying, goals can be reached because there is always an answer!

132

Impressum

Angaben gemäß § 5 TMG

© Richard Geiger 2019

1. Auflage

Richard Geiger

Borkenerstr. 60

48653 Coesfeld

Covergestaltung: Fiverr

Coverfoto: depositphotos.com

Wir sind nicht bereit oder verpflichtet, an

Streitbeilegungsverfahren vor

einerVerbraucherschlichtungsstelle teilzunehmen.

CPSIA information can be obtained
at www.ICGtesting.com
Printed in the USA
LVHW081806190420
654025LV00015B/2702